READY, SET, DRAW!

ANIMALS

AILIN CHAMBERS

W

FRANKLIN WATTS
LONDON • SYDNEY

Aberdeenshire

3168632

First published in 2015 by Franklin Watts

Copyright © Arcturus Holdings Limited

Franklin Watts
338 Euston Road
London
NW1 3BH

Franklin Watts Australia
Level 17/207 Kent Street, Sydney, NSW 2000

Produced by Arcturus Publishing Limited,
26/27 Bickels Yard, 151–153 Bermondsey Street, London SE1 3HA

All rights reserved.

The right of Ailin Chambers to be identified as the author of this work
has been asserted by him in accordance with the Copyright, Designs and
Patents Act 1988.

Editors: Samantha Hilton, Kate Overy and Joe Harris
Illustrations: Dynamo Limited
Design concept: Keith Williams
Design: Dynamo Limited and Notion Design
Cover design: Ian Winton

A CIP catalogue record for this book is available
from the British Library.

Dewey Decimal Classification Number 743.6
ISBN 978 1 4451 4185 5

Printed in China

SL003590UK

Supplier 03, Date 1214, Print run 3883

ABERDEENSHIRE LIBRARIES	
3168632	
Bertrams	24/07/2015
J743.6	£7.99

CONTENTS

GRAB THESE!

Are you ready to create some amazing pictures? Wait a minute! Before you begin drawing, you will need a few important pieces of equipment.

PENS AND PENCILS

You can use a variety of drawing tools including pens, chalks, pencils and paints. But to begin with use an ordinary HB pencil.

PAPER

Use a clean sheet of paper for your final drawings. Scrap paper is useful and cheap for your practice work.

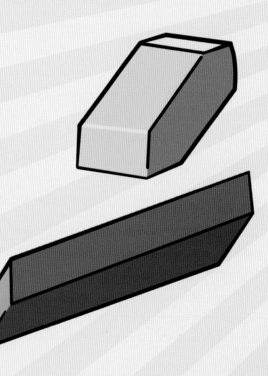

ERASERS

Everyone makes mistakes! That's why every artist has a good eraser. When you rub out a mistake, do it gently. Scrubbing hard at your paper will ruin your drawing and possibly even rip it.

RULER

Always use a ruler to draw straight lines.

COMPASS

You can use a compass to draw a perfect circle. However, some people find this tricky. Try drawing round a coin, bottle top or any other small, round item you can find.

INK LINES

The drawings in this book have been finished with ink lines to make them sharper and cleaner. You can get the same effect by using a ballpoint or felt-tip pen.

PAINT

Adding colour to your drawing brings it to life. You can use felt-tip pens, coloured pencils or water-based paints such as poster paints, which are easy to clean.

GETTING STARTED

In this book we use a simple two-colour system to show you how to draw a picture. Just remember: new lines are blue lines!

STARTING WITH STEP 1

The first lines you will draw are very simple shapes. They will be shown in blue, like this. You should draw them with a normal HB pencil.

ADDING MORE DETAIL

As you move on to the next step, the lines you have already drawn will be shown in black. The new lines for that stage will appear in blue.

FINISHING YOUR PICTURE

When you reach the final stage you will see the image in full colour with a black ink line. Inking a picture means tracing the main lines with a black pen. After the ink dries, use your eraser to remove all the pencil lines before adding your colour.

HAPPY

Draw wide-open eyes and raised eyebrows to create a happy face.

EMOTIONS

Once you've learned how to draw the animals in this book, you might want to try drawing them with different expressions. They could look happy, sad, angry or even puzzled.

ANGRY

Add straight lines for eyebrows, an open mouth and a jagged line for teeth. Now he looks angry!

SURPRISED

Big eyes and one raised eyebrow, together with a round mouth, help your bear to look surprised.

SAD

By curving the bear's eyebrows and mouth down, you can make him look sad.

THINKING

A pointed eyebrow and a slightly wobbly mouth make him look as if he is thinking about something.

EYES

As you can see, it's very easy to change expressions with a few tweaks. You can completely alter your character by just changing the eyes and eyebrows.

Here are a few to try. From the top, these eyes are: surprised, sleepy, scared, angry and sneaky.

GORILLA

A gorilla is the world's largest ape. It has a large head and its arms are longer than its legs. It often walks on all fours.

STEP 1

First, draw a simple shape that looks like a table tennis bat.

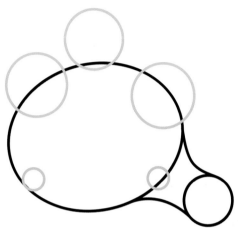

STEP 2

Next, add five circles to form the base for the gorilla's shoulders and elbows.

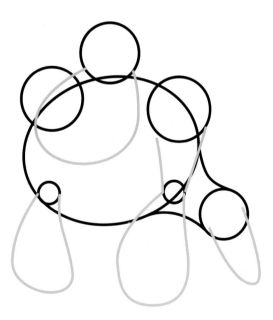

STEP 3

Now, add five more shapes to make the powerful arms, one leg and large jaw.

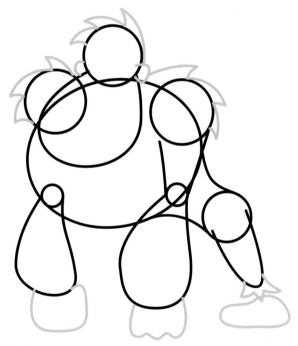

STEP 4

Draw small spikes to create the hair on the gorilla's head and shoulders. Don't forget to draw its hands and feet.

SUPER TIP!

The gorilla's face may look complicated but it starts with three simple steps...

- The eyebrows

- The eyes

- The nose

STEP 5

Add more fur to the arms. Draw simple lines for your gorilla's face, lip, chest, toes and back leg.

STEP 6

Colour in your gorilla using two shades of the same colour. You could use blue, grey or brown.

PONY

A pony is a small horse with short legs, a strong, stocky body, and a long mane and tail. Follow these step-by-step instructions to create your very own pony.

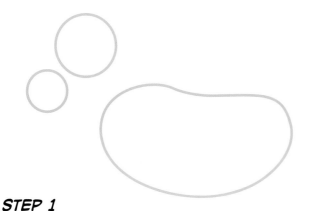

STEP 1

Start with two circles and a jelly bean shape to give you the pony's head and body.

STEP 2

Link the three shapes together and add a circle and an oval shape for the tops of the pony's legs.

STEP 3

Next, add six small circles for the leg and hoof joints. Draw an ear and the top of the pony's mane.

STEP 4

Draw lines to link the leg and hoof joints to create the pony's legs. Add nostrils, an eyelid and the front part of the mane.

STEP 5

Draw the long, bushy mane and tail. Add hooves, complete its eye and eyebrow, then add its other ear.

STEP 6

You can colour your pony any shade you like. Dapples, as shown here, are a nice touch.

PANDA

A panda is a large black and white bear with a thick, woolly coat. It lives in the forests of China and spends most of its time eating bamboo.

STEP 1

Draw a large oval shape, slightly narrower at the top, to make your panda's body.

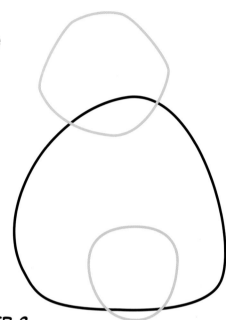

STEP 2

Add one oval shape to make the panda's head and another for its leg.

STEP 3

Next, add curved lines to make the panda's arms, ears and an outstretched leg.

STEP 4

A panda's feet look a lot like shoes. Large circles on its face make the eye patches. Add a small nose.

STEP 5

Add a smiling face, eyebrows, eyes, claws and its favourite food – a stick of bamboo. See the Super Tip to find out how to draw bamboo.

SUPER TIP!

A stick of bamboo is very simple to draw.

- Draw a straight-edged rectangle like this.

- Pencil in the lines for the bamboo segments.

- When you ink the picture, add curves between the lines. This will make the bamboo look bumpy and ridged.

STEP 6

Real pandas are black and white… but who says yours has to be? Why not try some other colours – purple and pink, or green and orange?

13

SHARK

A shark is a big fish with a smooth, streamlined body and powerful fins that help it to glide swiftly through the water.

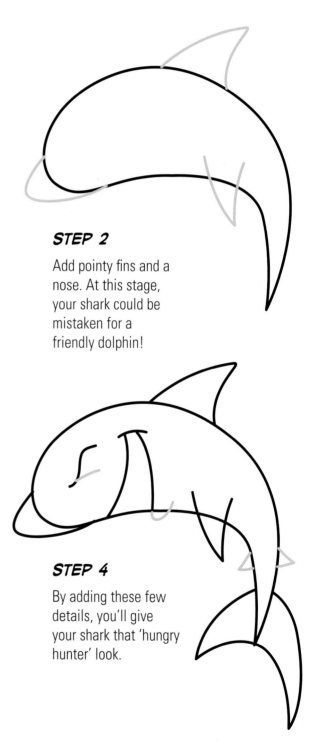

STEP 1

Draw a large teardrop shape to make the shark's sleek body.

STEP 2

Add pointy fins and a nose. At this stage, your shark could be mistaken for a friendly dolphin!

STEP 3

Next, draw a large, wide mouth, a squiggle for its eye and a large tail fin.

STEP 4

By adding these few details, you'll give your shark that 'hungry hunter' look.

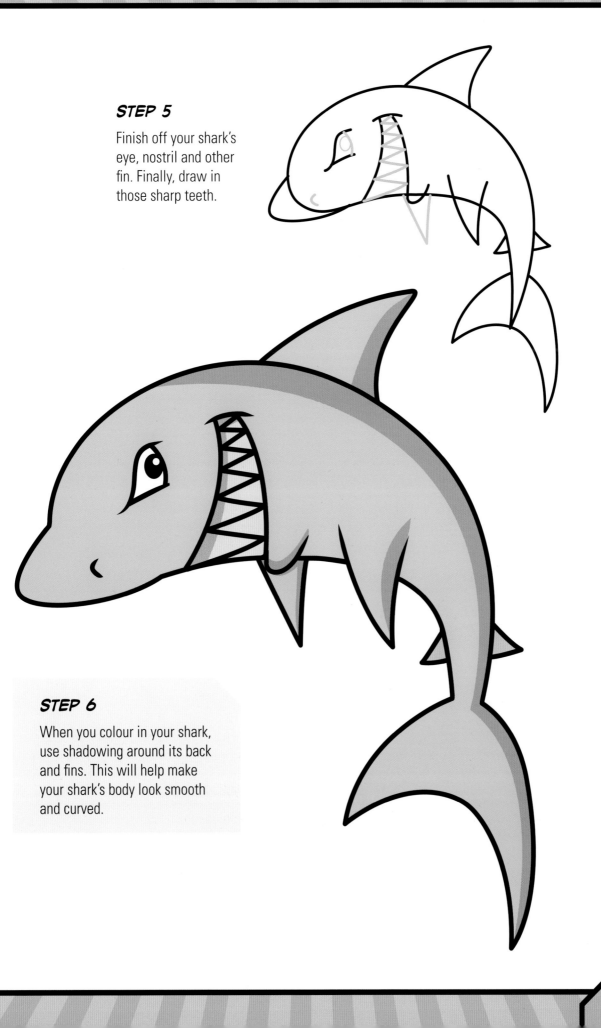

STEP 5

Finish off your shark's
eye, nostril and other
fin. Finally, draw in
those sharp teeth.

STEP 6

When you colour in your shark,
use shadowing around its back
and fins. This will help make
your shark's body look smooth
and curved.

RATTLESNAKE

A rattlesnake is a large snake with a rattle at the end of its tail. When it's surprised or about to attack, it coils its long body, rears up its head, and shakes its rattle loudly!

STEP 1

First, draw two long, squashed sausage shapes to make the coils of your rattlesnake's body.

STEP 2

Add two curved lines that meet at the top to make the rattlesnake's long neck.

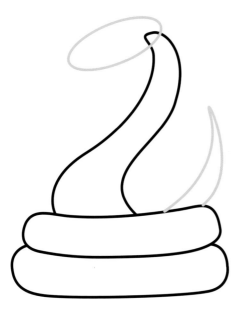

STEP 3

For the rattlesnake's head, draw a wide, oval shape. Then add a long, pointy tail.

STEP 4

Next, add two 'eyebrow' shapes on its head. Draw a line down one side of its neck and a small circle to create an extra coil.

SUPER TIP!

A really simple way to draw the snake's famous rattle is to build it from squashed sausages (just like its body).

Add sausage shapes to the tail, making each one smaller as you get closer to the tip of the rattlesnake's tail.

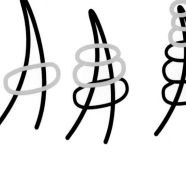

STEP 5

Complete its face and add a long, forked tongue. Draw V-shapes to show the snake's markings. You can colour these in a different shade.

STEP 6

To make the eye look really snake-like, simply draw a vertical line inside the eyeball. Then add some colours.

GRIZZLY BEAR

A grizzly is a huge bear with thick, brown fur and a slightly flattened face. It has large, powerful paws and very long, sharp claws!

STEP 1

First, draw a squashed egg shape to make your bear's tubby body.

STEP 2

Add the bear's feet. Then, draw a rough diamond shape for its head.

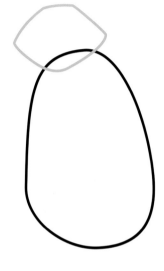

STEP 3

Now it's time to start building the bear's body. Add arms, legs, ears and nose with these simple shapes.

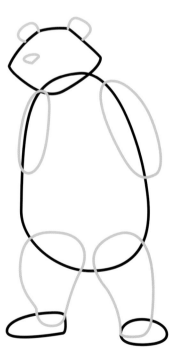

STEP 4

Finish off the bear's arms with two more shapes. Then add a long brow and muzzle.

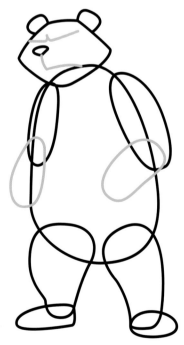

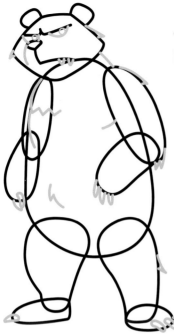

STEP 5

Next, add your bear's eyes, sharp claws and teeth.

STEP 6

Finally, don't forget its thick brown fur. See the Super Tip below to help you.

SUPER TIP!

To make drawing fur on animals simple, follow the rule of 'less is more'. You will save yourself a lot of time by not overcrowding your drawing with too much detail.

- Draw the line of the body shape smoothly like this.

- Use jagged lines like these in some parts of the outline to hint at the body shape being covered in fur.

- To give a large area a furry texture, you only have to draw a few small zigzag-shaped fur marks, rather than covering the whole body.

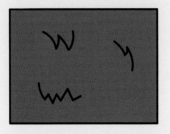

TIGER

A tiger is the largest of the big cats. Its orange and black stripy body helps it to blend perfectly into its jungle surroundings.

STEP 1

Start by drawing a rectangle and a circle. Link them together with two curved lines.

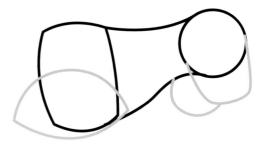

STEP 2

Add these three shapes to create the main part of the tiger's head and its back legs.

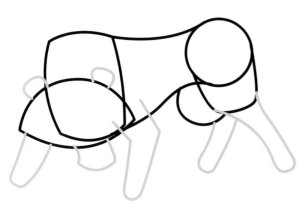

STEP 3

Add a pair of ears to the top of its head and draw in the legs. The small shape at the bottom of the tiger's head will be its lower jaw.

STEP 4

Next, draw the eyes, nose, muzzle, feet and tail. Make sure you draw its tail using curved lines with no sharp angles.

SUPER TIP!

Start the tiger's stripes with simple single lines. You can use straight lines, curved lines or zigzags. Then draw lines on either side of that first line to make the shapes shown here.

STEP 5

Add eyelids and eyes to complete the tiger's face. If you want your tiger to look more friendly, draw the eyelids higher up its face. Draw simple lines for its stripes. See the Super Tip to find out how to make them work.

STEP 6

Colour your tiger a nice bright orange and strong black.

KITTEN

A kitten is a young cat with soft fur, a large head, big eyes and ears and a long tail. Kittens are playful and make popular pets.

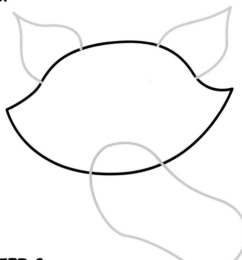

STEP 1

First, draw a shape a bit like a lemon. A kitten's head is big compared to the rest of its body.

STEP 2

Add two large ears on top and a fat sausage shape to create your kitten's body.

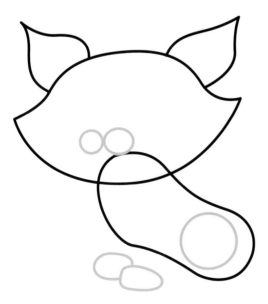

STEP 3

Next, add a large circle for the back leg, two small ones for the face and two ovals for the front paws.

STEP 4

Draw two large eyes. Then, add a little nose and complete the back leg and front legs.

Your kitten doesn't have to be the same colour as this one. As you can see, a simple colour change gives your furry friend a completely different look.

Why not colour a few of them in different colours and have a whole litter of cuddly, fluffy kittens?

STEP 5

Now fill in the final details. Add eyes, eyebrows, a small mouth, fur around the ears and cheeks, and don't forget a long, swishy tail.

STEP 6

Your cat can be any colour. Adding small white spots in the eyes will give them a cute, shiny effect.

PUPPY

A puppy is a young dog with a furry body and large paws. When it's happy or excited, a puppy wags its tail from side to side. Puppies make popular pets.

STEP 1

Start by drawing a simple circle. If you like, you could trace around a coin.

STEP 2

Then, add a big, squashy jelly-bean shape to make the puppy's body.

STEP 3

Four more circular shapes will make the muzzle and feet.

STEP 4

Draw curved front legs to make it look as if your puppy is about to jump up. Add a back leg. Draw big, floppy ears and a large nose on its muzzle.

STEP 5

Next, draw on its big eyes and its mouth with a slobbery tongue. Then, complete the paws and other back leg. Finally, don't forget its waggly tail!

STEP 6

You can choose any pattern you like for your puppy's body. You could try some large patches, or small spots, like you see on Dalmatians.

PARROT

A parrot is a bird with brightly coloured feathers and a large, curved beak.

STEP 1

First, draw a slightly wobbly pear shape to make the parrot's body.

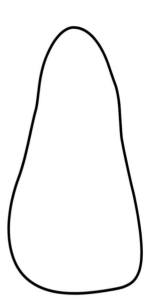

STEP 2

Next, add simple wing shapes and a large hooked beak.

STEP 3

Add the long, curved claws and a large eye. Then draw some plumage on top of your parrot's head.

SUPER TIP!

You don't have to draw every feather on a parrot's body. If you want to make it look like it has feathers all over, just draw some little patches of feather shapes. They should be spaced out over its body and wings.

STEP 4

Add in the branch and a bit more detail on the eye.

STEP 5

Give the parrot some long tail feathers. Then add more feathers over the body. They look a bit like the number '3' lying on its side.

STEP 6

Now you can colour your parrot in nice, bright colours.

A wolf is a wild animal with a large head, long legs, big paws and a thick, furry coat. Wolves hunt other animals and they have strong jaws filled with sharp teeth.

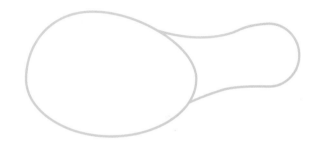

STEP 1

First, draw a large egg shape to make the wolf's hunched shoulders. Then add a longer shape to make its body.

STEP 2

Draw another smaller oval to make the wolf's head. Then add the top of its front leg, top of the back leg and a thick, bushy tail.

STEP 3

Add ears, the lower jaw and paws to the front leg. Then, follow the lines for the back legs as shown here and you won't go wrong.

STEP 4

Add a muzzle and nose to the wolf's face. Draw in another front paw, back paw and begin to draw some its fur.

STEP 5

Complete the wolf's eyes, add the last paw and then draw in some more fur.

STEP 6

Grey tones will give your wolf a scary look. Use a light grey on the underside of its body, its chin and the tip of its tail.

GLOSSARY

ape A type of large animal with a hairy body and no tail that is closely related to monkeys and humans. Apes include chimpanzees, gorillas and gibbons.

bamboo A kind of giant grass, with lots of tough, hollow stems.

Dalmatian A type of large dog with black spots and patches on a white coat.

dapples Rounded patches of different colours on an animal's coat.

HB pencil A pencil with a lead that is neither hard nor soft, but somewhere in between.

muzzle The nose and mouth of an animal such as a horse or dog.

plumage The feathers of a bird.

stocky Broad and sturdy.

vertical Describes something that goes up and down (rather than across).

FURTHER READING

Draw 50 Animals by Lee J. Ames (Watson-Guptill, 2012)

How to Draw Animals: A Step-by-Step Guide to Animal Art by Peter Gray (Arcturus, 2013)

How to Draw Animals in Simple Steps by Various Authors (Search Press, 2011)

WEBSITES

www.activityvillage.co.uk/learn-to-draw-animals

www.howtodrawanimals.net

www.wedrawanimals.com

INDEX